ENDURING, SHARING, LOVING

ABOUT THE ALDER CENTRE

'For all those affected by the death of a child'

The Alder Centre is a pioneering project established by a small group of health care professionals in partnership with bereaved parents. It is in the grounds of the Royal Liverpool Children's Hospital, Alder Hey – the largest children's hospital in Europe. The Centre has the support of the hospital trust. However, some of its costs have to be met from voluntary funds. Proceeds from this book will help to maintain the services provided by the Alder Centre.

The Centre recognises that the effects of a child's death extend far beyond the immediate family and include all those who have been involved in the child's care. It provides counselling and support for anyone who is affected by the death of a child.

Full-time staff work with volunteer parents who know and understand bereavement first-hand. Together they are there to comfort and, perhaps most important of all, to listen.

Although the Alder Centre has no religious affiliation, the value of encouraging the bereaved to explore their own beliefs and find their own truths is recognised.

ENDURING, SHARING, LOVING

For All Those Affected by the Death of a Child

Edited by Marilyn Shawe

Foreword by Grace Sheppard

DARTON, LONGMAN AND TODD
LONDON
in association with
THE ALDER CENTRE

First published in 1992 by
Darton, Longman and Todd Ltd
89 Lillie Road, London SW6 1UD

in association with

the Alder Centre
Royal Liverpool Children's Hospital
Alder Hey
Eaton Road, Liverpool L12 2AP

ISBN 0–232–52010–0

A catalogue record for this book is available from the British Library

Cover: photo by Graham Topping; design by Elizabeth Ayer
Text design by Sandie Boccacci

Phototypeset in 10/11½pt Ehrhardt by Intype, London
Printed and bound in Great Britain
at the University Press, Cambridge

CONTENTS

Foreword by Grace Sheppard

Preface by Marilyn Shawe

Hell is not all fire and brimstone,
It is being separated from
those we love.

Heaven is not the vague hope of eternal bliss,
It is the belief that we will be reunited
with those we love.

Dedicated to all our children we have lost.

FOREWORD

When a child dies, we are all affected. A life full of newness and promise is cut short. But no one feels the pain more than the parents. Their whole world is shattered, and disturbing questions arise to haunt and to taunt them. Why? What have I done to deserve this? Where is God now? These questions lead on to feelings of guilt and lostness, anger and despair which are deeply troubling. They can leave a person feeling isolated and disorientated, and, if not attended to, can cripple relationships for life.

Because of the impact of the shock, these strong feelings are more active, and need an outlet. Anyone affected by the death of a child needs to tell another person how they feel to rediscover their own sense of proportion. The emotional bruising and pain is deep and needs plenty of time to heal. The healing can begin when those destructive frightening feelings are recognised and allowed out of the system. It helps just to talk. So someone needs to be there to listen. No one is needed to preach or dish out the advice or judgement. And 'jollying along' is the last thing to do.

As well as talking there are other ways of expression, and writing is one of them. For some, prayer, spoken or written, helps. This anthology of writings compiled by Marilyn Shawe, whose daughter died aged twelve, gives us a chance to listen to how it feels. She has divided the book into three sections: Enduring the Pain; Sharing the Loss; Loving our Children. Mothers, like Marilyn, and fathers, a grandmother, sisters, friends, a teacher and hospital staff, have contributed poems and thoughts from the depths of their being. We are privileged to be entrusted with those.

As well as having the courage to express themselves frankly and honestly they have also given us a gift. By sharing themselves so truthfully and eloquently, they enable us to increase our understanding of how it is. After reading this book, I believe I am wiser, and better equipped to be a more sensitive listener and friend. I have been touched to see how many of the writers express a faith in something beyond themselves. Some have named the name of God and Christ, and others have not. Either way, many have found strength to carry on from that kind of believing.

For those who have recently been affected by the death of a child, this book brings hope and comfort. Dipping into it, they will feel less alone in their grief, and discover the warmth of belonging to a body of people who have been there too. It could be the trigger of freedom, when a person finds that the moment has come when they feel brave enough to begin to talk or even write, and let the tears flow. A new awareness of feeling understood and accepted in the middle of darkness, confusion and pain will emerge. Fears will begin to slacken their grip and new life will return.

We do not help ourselves prepare for death of any kind by banishing it to a place where it is talked about in whispers and in private as if it were something to be ashamed of. If we were more open with one another in ordinary conversation about our own fears of death and dying, then those who then have to sustain the shock of losing a child in death might feel better able to talk more freely. This anthology is a beginning, and I warmly recommend it. If it helps one person, then the death of a precious child will bring new life to another, and will not have been in vain.

Grace Sheppard
Bishop's Lodge
Liverpool

PREFACE

In helping to produce the monthly newsletter for the Alder Centre, I was moved by the many poems and letters that we received from families about the love and devotion they expressed for their children, and their fierce determination to make something positive come out of a terrible tragedy.

The something positive is this book. It is an anthology of verse and prose which reflects people's struggles to accept the unacceptable, the death of their child. It provides an insight into the supreme joy that our children bring to us, the depths of despair and anguish when we suffer their loss, but ultimately the power of enduring love that transcends even death.

The first section of this book, 'Enduring the Pain', may be painful to read but it acknowledges the extreme extent of people's emotions following the death of a beloved child and gives them a much needed outlet. It is a purely honest approach about our immediate reactions to bereavement and grief. It is almost primeval in its basic instincts about the fierce protective love we as humans have for our young ones. It covers feelings of disbelief, anger, anguish, initial grief, despair, addressing God and the desperation of searching for reasons and answers to the unanswerable. Even though we are brought face to face with pain and death there is an optimism inside us which keeps us hanging on by our fingertips to the belief in immortality.

The second section, 'Sharing the Loss', explores our need to talk about what has happened, to tell someone about our loss, to confide in a caring listener about how much it hurts. There is a need to express feelings to others, to share inescapable grief and sadness, to reassure ourselves that we are not going mad because we need to say again and again how we feel. The questioning to God about '*Why* did this happen to my child?' and the receiving of no satisfactory answer is one of the biggest sources of agony and frustration to many parents. We share our grief and our letting go, our precious memories of special times, and our holding on (to faith, to hope, to sanity, to life). We learn to face the unalterable fact that life goes on.

'Loving our Children' is a glorious tribute to the children themselves. It is about the gift of sheer joy and happiness which children bring to us unconditionally. It is about our admiration for their courage and bravery throughout an illness, or about the fine example they set us, or in the case of still births and cot deaths explaining how precious and loved they were even though they were here for so short a time. It is the fear of our dead children being forgotten, as though they never existed, which brings so much pain to parents. This section of the book gives rein to our need to love them still. It is about the poignancy of never seeing those children again but also the certainty that they will remain in our hearts for ever. It is about joy and happiness, faith, hope and love, and the specialness of all our children.

Marilyn Shawe
Alder Centre

PART ONE

ENDURING THE PAIN

For a parent who loses a child an abyss of pain opens up and it appears eternal. I cannot find words to describe this pain but will just say that it is physical as well as mental and emotional. It incorporates virtually every emotional feeling you can think of from apathy to agoraphobia.

Jo Edwards

Regrettably society is not conditioned to come to terms with the death of children. But children do die and the pain of it can destroy the lives of those left behind. Without assistance many couples can become totally submerged by the waves of grief that continue to ebb and flow for longer than those mercifully untouched by the death of a child can ever know. Most experts feel that the loss of a child produces a permanent bereavement . . . 'Grief returns with the revolving year' was the poet Shelley's sentiment.

David Dodman

DISBELIEF

NO MORE?

My child
How can it be
That you who were a living
Breathing part of me
Are no more?

Suddenly
Without warning
You closed your eyes
And shut us out
For ever!

My child
And I had no choice
In this matter.
Inexplicably
You died.

Helplessly
I watched you go
In disbelief.
I was totally
Impotent.

Marilyn Shawe

IT'S ONLY A DREAM

I woke up this morning and thought, what a lovely day, the sun is shining, the black clouds have gone and I feel no pain any more in my heart. As I turn I see my baby looking up and smiling at me. I never thought the day would come when we could take

3

Kevin home with us. All those days and nights at the hospital don't seem so bad anymore.

Anthony comes in and kisses Kevin, he's so happy now that he has a playmate. I pick him up and hold him in my arms but his Dad and Anthony want to hold him as well, all four of us get into bed. We kiss and cuddle one another, we sing and play. I never thought we could be so happy as we are now. I love the sound of laughter from children playing.

We seem to have been playing for hours, I lay my head on the pillow for a few minutes with my eyes closed. When I open them it's dark again, the pain is back once more.

> Please, no it can't be, but it is,
> the same dream I've had before.

Ann Scotland

BIRTH AND DEATH

In the pain and fear of giving birth
I watched you come into this world
With awe and wonder in my heart
Then I held you in my arms and cried.

In the pain and fear of impending death
I watched you go out of this world
With shock and disbelief in my heart
Then I held you in my arms and cried.

In the pain and fear of bereavement
I've searched for you in this world
With anguish and grief in my heart
Then I held the memory of you in my arms
... and cried ... and cried.

Marilyn Shawe

4

ANGER

TRAPPED

My grief is like an animal trapped deep within my heart,
When awake it roars and roars and tears my world apart.
Even when it sleeps it quietly moans and sighs,
That makes me very sad and always makes me cry.

But worst of all is the night.
When dreams are many and sleep is light, I relive that
    awful night
So many times again.

Back comes all the sorrow, the anger and the pain,
The memories of my son are with me night and day.
Will this animal in my heart ever go away?

Heather Parry

A GREEDY FOE

Death you are a greedy foe
You plunder those we love,
Ruthless as a bird of prey,
You swoop down from above.

Death you have no remorse,
You just throw your weight about,
You don't heed the pain you cause,
You are a bully and a lout.

Death you are a part of life,
And yet when you come life's done.
The old and weary may be glad to meet you,
But not children who have scarce begun.

5

Death you last for ever,
But life has so short a span,
Adam what curse you left us
In the garden where life began.

Death you came too soon to us,
You sneaked up like a thief,
Taking our most precious daughter,
Whose life was much too brief.

Death when God chose you,
To repay man's original sin,
What gave you the right to execute
At random for a whim.

Death there must be a reason
Why you're so free and wild,
You are more evil than the Devil
To separate a mother from her child.

Marilyn Shawe

THE KNOWING

Did you know the child you lost,
Your child who died, still lives?
And do you know just where he is,
Inside the heart that gives?

In disbelief we turn away
When death knocks at our door
Rejecting life as valueless
Rejecting faith once more.

Why do our children have to die?
Why us? Why us?, we cry.
It isn't fair, what have we done?
He didn't say goodbye.

6

I can't believe it is a test,
A lesson I must live.
The bad news is my son is dead,
There's no worse news to give.

Don't tell me time will heal my pain.
It won't, as well I know,
And I don't want to live right now.
I'm angry, LET ME GO.

Clare Corner

ANGUISH

SAYING GOODBYE

That last night by your bed, in armchairs we sat. It was so hard to believe, after almost eleven years of nightly disturbances, this was to be the last time I would be required to attend to you.

You lay in my arms the night through. I scanned the screens, and the faces of the players, as the last act in your wonderful journey of life was coming to its end. I could feel your warmth and weight, but as tightly as I held, I couldn't make you stay. I felt so desolate and angry as your life ebbed away.

I cannot love again, the way I loved you. I want to follow you. Where have you gone? I'm searching, I'm searching. Show me the way.

I couldn't say goodbye to you the way I wanted to, the way I needed to. We were like Cathy and Heathcliffe, you and I. Mountains should have shook and the earth tremble. But I could only look into your eyes, smile and say 'good luck'. It's so hard to smile when your heart is breaking.

John Gosney

WHEN I MISS YOU MOST

When I'm making up the packed lunches for school
and your yellow box with the picture of the Muppets isn't there
   ... That's when I miss you.

When I'm pegging out the clothes
and your favourite sweatshirt with Mickey Mouse on
is not flapping around with the others ... That's when I miss
   you.

When we go to the dentist
and he calls out all our names one by one, except yours ...
   That's when I miss you.

When I'm setting the table for tea
and your place is empty . . . That's when I miss you.

When the ice-cream man comes round
and I buy everyone their favourite ice, and I can't buy one for
    you . . . That's when I miss you.

When I tip-toe into the bedrooms at night
and kiss the others goodnight . . . your pillow is empty . . . That's
    when I miss you.

When I am sad and lonely
and nothing else will do except to have you back
and hear you say 'I love you mum' . . . That's when I miss you
    most of all.

Marilyn Shawe

INSIDE OUT

We thought our sons immortal,
Oh! we knew one day they'd die,
But never thought we'd be the ones
To sit beside a marble stone
And ask each other why.

All our hopes and dreams for Tom
Are neatly folded up and stored away,
And only taken out to look at and think about,
Never to be used again.

I'm crying on the inside
And laughing on the out,
I'm talking on the outside
But deep inside I shout,
What would you think of me
If I turned inside out?

Dave Sutton

A SAD GOODBYE

Hearts torn to shreds, the pain never goes,
Our minds try to clutch at our life as it was,
Eyes filled with tears see things differently now.
Hands ache to touch, and arms to embrace,
The chance just to hold him and kiss him goodbye.
Ears strain to hear his laugh, filled with joy.
Echoes of sadness, resound in my head.
Things that seemed real don't seem there any more.
People we loved cannot reach us today,
Jesus, watch over our treasure, we pray,
Enjoy him as we did, those short happy years,
Carry our sorrow, we can't bear it alone.

Maureen Prescott

ALWAYS NEAR

A lifetime of tears lies ahead
But I can stand the pain.
I want to suffer again and again.
My life is pointless without Clare
But through this suffering
She is always near.

John Gosney

BE THERE

Send me no false comfort
Just of words
– The endless plastic platitudes
On which your towers of defence are built.

Spare me from your well-meaning attempts
To minimise my discomfort
Which activates your own, however buried.

10

Spare me your echoing distance
As you withdraw into a safe place
Shielding yourself from the shrapnel
Of a broken heart.

Protect me from your jocularity
And Butlins smiles and waves
For they mock the gravity of the situation
And do little to reach the turmoil underneath.

Save me from your own discomfort
And awareness at my pain
For it is real, and part of my reality
Now but not for always.

Just be there as a person
Gently hold my hand and listen
For there is solace in the merest touch
And comfort in the knowledge of your presence.

Anna McKenzie

GRIEF

TO LOSE A CHILD

Grief is the loneliest of all human experiences
Losing a child is the hardest thing in life to bear
There is no antidote,
No cure,
No end,
No one has any answers.

It is a long hard battle,
But there are no enemies.
It is a long and winding path,
But there are no signs to guide you.
It is an overbearing weight,
But no one can see the burden that you carry in your heart.
It is unimaginable anguish,
But no one else perceives the half of it.
It is the saddest of all deaths,
But the world is overflowing with enough sadness of its own.
It is the end of your world,
But you have to go on living.

Marilyn Shawe

A MOUNTAIN TO CLIMB

I've had a break from the pain these last couple of days, and the
relief is something totally unlooked for, or expected. It's not that
I am happy, or even remotely at ease, but the suffocating, immense
weight has been lifted from me, and I am now in a limbo of
nothingness, where maybe I can recharge myself ready for the
next assault.

A mountain to climb, a marathon to run. Each day brings its
test of your ability to survive. You have to cope with the smiles
and the small talk that make up ordinary everyday life for others.

For convention's sake you pretend that you are like that too. But on the inside you roar like a caged lion. At least at the end of the day you can think, 'Well, that's another one out of the way'.

John Gosney

MY TIME WITH YOU

They say that time will ease the pain
But grief will last much longer,
I only know that I loved her so
And the memories grow stronger.

There's an emptiness inside me
A void that can't be filled,
There's a hope for a life hereafter
And a love that can't be killed.

There's a bond that can't be broken
Forged throughout the years,
These feelings deep within me
Won't be washed away by tears.

Allan Brigden

A PROCESS?

It must have been a psychologist who invented the clinically slick term of 'the grieving process'.

What a ludicrously inappropriate phrase to define the mental, physical and emotional turmoil that you are left to sort out after your child has died. I can think of no other trauma in life which is so crudely and ineptly called a process. Not a puberty process, not a post-natal depression process, not a menopausal process, or even a mid-life process. Not even birth or death is called a process.

The 'grieving process' conveys nothing other than a mechanical method of accounting for certain stages in grief. It implies that it is a continual going forward in an orderly progressive way.

Nothing could be less true.

Grieving takes no account of an orderly disciplined progress. It is erratic and chooses its own winding path which may make as many diversions, detours and circuits as it needs.

Why do we allow our deepest feelings to be sterilised by a meaningless label such as 'the grieving process'?

Why don't we stop trying to compartmentalise grief and call it what it really is – 'learning to live with death'.

Marilyn Shawe

GUILTY?

I am writing this on on one of my down days. Why am I writing this? I don't know. How do I feel? Guilty.

Guilty about what? Guilty that I am alive and my beautiful grandson, Anthony, is dead. Guilty because my daughter Julie, Anthony's mummy, is ill, torn apart by grief.

Guilty that my husband lays seriously ill in a coma, after suffering a cardiac arrest eleven months after the death of Anthony, again caused by grief.

Guilty because my other daughter, Helen, who was six months pregnant at the time her dad took ill, lost her little boy, Liam. Once again the cause was grief.

I felt nothing. No pain, no shock, absolutely nothing. Why did I feel nothing? I don't know, because my daughter was devastated. I do remember saying to myself, 'I am not going to get hurt again, I am not going to let anyone hurt me again, ever'. Was I wrong to think in that way? I just don't know.

Guilty because after Anthony died I sought out help for myself. For the first time in my life, I put myself before anyone else. Why? Because I was in so much pain, I couldn't help anyone else.

Guilty because I saw their grief and the pain in their eyes, and I couldn't help them. Guilty because I was in a world of my own, and I didn't want anyone to share that world.

Guilty because I had found a haven at the Alder Centre, a haven where I found peace. I felt protected, a haven where I knew nobody would hurt me, a haven where I could shed my tears and nobody would say, 'You have got to be strong for Bill and the girls'.

Guilty because I didn't want to be strong for anyone but myself. I did find that strength from the Alder Centre, from the guidance, love and understanding which counsellors and bereaved parents gave me.

Guilty because I did find that inner strength. The strength I needed to help my family. Guilty because my help came too late to help them. Guilty about my mixed feelings towards God. Guilty on days like today when I am feeling down, I don't want to shower, comb my hair, put make-up on and dress smart the way my family and friends like to see me.

Guilty because I want to look and dress like a tramp, a drop-out, with a big shattered heart around my neck, and say to people, 'Look at me, what you see on the outside is what I feel on the inside'.

Guilty because that is what I feel today. Tomorrow is another story.

Diane Bayliss

TEARS ON MY PILLOW

Is it only four weeks since I kissed you goodbye, my big brother? Dear, my heart still aches and my tears still flow as I lie here, my pillow getting wetter and wetter through the night.

Mum's voice comes to me, I hear her crying out, 'I did not think I would see my son die ... see my son die'. Over and over I hear her saying it.

I feel my heart pounding, my stomach feels as if I've been kicked inside out. 'How', I ask myself, 'must my mother be bearing the pain?' I feel the hurt so much, how can she go on? Yet she does.

When I see her I cannot cry because she looks so lost. I know she is thinking of her son, not the grown man as he was when he died, but her baby son and the little boy with scraped knees. The boy who became school champion at sports and the boy who became the father figure to his two younger sisters after their

15

father died. All these thoughts will be going through her head as she recalls all the happy memories of her son.

Yet we cannot help each other as the pain is so fierce that we are unable to speak aloud for fear of upsetting one another. So for me my pillow is my companion as I remember all my happy times we shared together as children. Sometimes I envy my brother because he will have seen my dad again. I have not seen him since I was seven years old and even then it was my pillow I turned to when I thought of my dad.

I have heard parents say that the brothers and sisters of the child that died don't seem to miss their brother or sister. All I can say is when you next make your child's bed, hold the pillow close to your cheeks and then you will know, yes they care, for there are tears on the pillow.

Frances Corlett

TEARDROPS KEEP FALLING

Teardrops keep falling from my eyes to my aching heart:
Teardrops keep falling, remembering the happy times to the sad times:
Teardrops keep falling, never knowing when they're going to stop:
They just keep falling: O Lord will they ever stop?
From morning to night time, teardrops keep falling.

Alison Moulder

16

DESPAIR

JUST LEAVE ME ALONE

I don't want to be reminded of what I've lost by seeing what you've got.

I don't want to be reminded of how sad I am by seeing how happy you are.

I need to be allowed to be me, and not be criticised for acting in a way you think I shouldn't.

Just leave me alone!

John Gosney

I THOUGHT I KNEW WHAT UNHAPPINESS MEANT

I had a sad life compared with some. Adopted at two, didn't like the mother who brought me up. The dad I loved died after a painful illness.

I thought I knew what unhappiness meant.

As time went by I found my birth mother in Mossley Hill and her sisters in the USA. They didn't want to know.

I thought I knew what unhappiness meant.

After eight years of searching, with the help of my friend Brenda, I found my natural father in Phoenix, Arizona ... five months too late.

I thought I knew what unhappiness meant.

I divorced, he was cruel to my children, Jeannie, Yvonne and myself.

I thought I knew what unhappiness meant.

My fifteen-year-old daughter Yvonne went on holiday to Spain on 14 September 1989. On 30 September at 8.33 p.m. the phone rang. My friends Jenny and Eric asked if they could come round

17

and see me. They came at 8.36 p.m. 'Lin, there has been an accident, *Yvonne has been killed*.' I could not believe my ears. 'There must be a mistake.' I was devastated. Many long hours later I arrived in the south of France and identified my beautiful daughter, Yvonne. There was no mistake.

Now I know what unhappiness means.

Lin Gunn

MISSING YOU

When it's misty and damp
And breath condenses,
That's when I miss you.
When it's cold and icy
And snow around
That's when I miss you.
When there is a freshness in the air
And new life starts to sprout,
That's when I miss you.
When it's warm and sunny
And everybody smiles,
That's when I miss you.

I've lost my direction, my ambition has gone,
What is the point of trying to go on,
Each day is much like the last,
The future is not important, only the past.

John Gosney

WHAT DOES IT MATTER?

What does it matter if my child is not bounding across the play
　　park with hair bobbing and cheeks aglow
As long as there are other children to swing the swings and
　　laugh and play.

18

Their multitude represents the future of mankind and covers
  up the gap that her death left.
Her presence is not missed any more by them.
What does it matter if she is not there?

What does it matter if she cannot feel the warmth of the sun
  on her skin
Or run through the spray of the surf and embrace the cool of
  the ocean.
As long as someone's children are there to enjoy the things that
  children do.
One less does not make any difference.
The world churns on without her.
What does it matter if she is not there?

What does it matter if Christmases come and go and she will
  never share them with us again,
Will never press her cheeks against the window pane
To see the first magical flakes of snow,
Will never wake sparkling eyed to see the celebrated morn.
As long as there are always children being born
Her leaving is compensated for.
What does it matter if she is not there?

It matters to me.
It matters because I love her and always will
And love means sharing her infectious love of life,
Feeling her pain,
Feeling her joy.
It matters because she was part of me
And now part of me has gone.
The part that loved the sun and sea and snow and waves
Does not sparkle for me any more.
All the smiling faces in the world don't smile for me
The way the sunshine of her smile lit up my heart.

Marilyn Shawe

ADDRESSING GOD

WHAT GOD CAN DO

I cannot curse
For what God's done
For he like me
Has lost a son . . .

But God invented Easter
He rolled away the stone
And resurrected Jesus Christ
So he wasn't left alone.

If God can do it once
To end his loss and pain
Why won't he wave his hand
And give us ours again?

Dave Sutton

DEAR LORD

I read in the Bible you wrought miracles
Heard you healed the sick, the lame and the blind.
When it came to saving common folk's loved ones
Why did you save some, but not mine?

I thought that hell was for sinners
Thought you cared for the weak and the mild.
I believed that you loved little children
Until the life was torn from my child.

How could you allow such terrible torment
On my daughter's small body to bear.
Illness ransacked her youth and her beauty
Leaving indignity, death and despair.

Surely it would have been more fitting
For a murderer or terrorist to die.
I could have seen the rough justice
If in hospital some criminal should lie.

The sun only shines on the righteous
I've heard other people say.
What did I do that was so wrong
To cause you to act in this way?

I loved her more than I loved you, Lord.
Is that the extent of my crime?
But if every mother was honest
Her child would come first every time.

To watch my little girl dying,
Is that how you thought I should pay?
Did you lay that fatal disease on her?
But on my heart was the burden you lay.

Don't tell me that I am guilty
For my daughter's death that day,
For I would have given my life gladly
If it had meant that she could stay.

Was it to make others fearful
That from righteousness not to stray?
Whatever I did that was wrong, Lord,
Her dying was too high a price to pay.

She never did any harm, Lord.
In fact she did mostly good.
She brightened our lives with her loving
And spread joy and happiness wherever she could.

If you are there and are listening
I think there's one thing you should explain.
When Jesus said 'suffer little children'
Did he mean with such anguish and pain?

21

I know that you lost your child too, Lord,
So you must understand this deep Hell.
But your son came back to be with you
And now you have my child as well.

It's so hard to go on without her.
It's the lovelight in her eyes that I miss
I'd give all the riches on earth, Lord,
Just to touch her once more with a kiss.

If you took her because you loved her
I can't really blame you for this,
But I love her deeply myself, Lord,
Without her there's just an abyss.

If only I knew she was happy
Not writhing in pain like on earth.
If she were set free from all suffering
More than life to me that is worth.

And so, dear Lord, there you have it,
You didn't really give me much choice.
I would have chosen for all children to be healthy
But do you listen to one small voice?

Marilyn Shawe

WHERE ARE YOU, GOD?

Why do some have to struggle against overwhelming odds?
Why do some pass the same way picking up happiness and joy
   with almost every step?
Where are you God? In this God-forsaken world.
Show yourself.
Are you compassion, are you love?
These are fragile, slender threads
I need to believe.
Show yourself.

John Gosney

22

A LETTER TO GOD

Lord, what is this strange life we've been thrown into? Where journeys never begin or end, just remain for ever, one foot in front of the other, like a weary soldier with no destination in sight, and no chance to go back. Did we ever belong in a world where time could be measured by happy weekends, and children safely asleep in their beds? Is that all a dream, or is this? I don't know.

I long so much for him just to be standing in front of me, gentle eyed and smiling, long so much for him that I could burst. Yet I would not dare touch him now in case he disappeared.

I know he's far safer with you than in this world of violence, drugs and Aids, but that doesn't mend the ugly open hole where my heart was. It is only covered with my clothes and no one but you could bear to look at it if it was uncovered. Lord, you know we love our other children just as much as him, but we seem to live a lie, trying to look normal for them, yet knowing it doesn't ring true. Would you please, in your mercy, take over where we are failing miserably, and let them know the truth?

I only have enough strength to put one foot in front of the other, but I do trust that you are leading us, and that you can see the end of the road. Even now I must begrudgingly admit that you are opening our eyes and understanding to a much wider horizon than we would normally have seen. Often you use the wild birds and butterflies, who seem to trust us implicitly. Even the flowers in the garden cry out, 'Kiss the joy, as it flies, don't cling to him or you will lose him; let him go free and he will never leave you.' Thank you for the precious little sparrow with the twisted foot who comes so close I'm sure it would eat out of our hands as the doves do; and thank you for the dove who chose to die peacefully, behind David's little magnolia bush last weekend.

No words in this world can touch my frozen heart, but you know how to start it melting. Father, help all who grieve, to open their eyes to the comfort you long to give them in their brokenness and give us grace to accept it, please.

Maureen Prescott

ONLY ONE MEMORY

Oh God!
What was so wrong?
What did I do?
To make you think Liam would be better with you?

We had our dreams,
A cheeky lad,
We would never have let him turn out bad.

You made a choice to give him life
Inside my womb, all warm and nice,
You let me feel his kicks and moves,
You let me see him dead and bruised.

I loved my son, but you gave me no time
To feel his tiny hand in mine,
Now all of the sorrow and all of the pain,
And only one memory to haunt me again and again.

His tightly closed eyes
His button nose,
How would he have grown, nobody knows.
You didn't give him a breath
And it was his right,
You never gave me time to kiss him goodnight.

Now all of the dreams and plans that I had
Are gone – never there. God was I so bad?
The memory only of the kicks and the moves,
And the last memory you left me was of him
Dead and bruised.

Helen Bayliss

SEARCHING

YOUR MELODY

The beautiful song that was you had vanished,
My world so empty when you had to go,
Never more to see your smiling face,
Never more to watch you grow.

At first I was too sad to hear you calling.
I wouldn't believe that you had gone,
Why was it that you had to leave us?
Why did I have to carry on?

But you were not content to watch us grieving,
You urged us on to search for you,
Your love was pouring down upon us,
Your music trying to play through.

Now once again we hear your music.
We know you haven't really gone.
The love we shared is never ending
Your melody will linger on.

Rose Foster

ONE YEAR LATER

I'd give my all to hear you say,
'Hello Mother, I'm home to stay'.
Your hand on my shoulder, your soft gentle touch,
Just one of the things that I miss so much.

Your 'never mind Mum', when nothing seemed right,
If I was upset you'd hold my hand tight.
Each day when you left me, and I watched you go,
You always looked back to wave 'Cheerio'.

I've learned to live on, though you are not here,
When left on my own I oft' shed a tear,
Thinking of things that I miss so much
Your hand on my shoulder, your soft gentle touch.

Janet Dickinson

BANK HOLIDAY BLUES

Half-heartedly preparing for a day out,
A picnic, a theme park, a country fair, it doesn't matter much,
I know what I will see,
Little girls with blue eyes and long blonde hair.

Happy families hand in hand,
Complete unto themselves,
Only serve to remind me of my loss,
We will never be complete again.
Fairground music, hot-dog stands,
Sunny days, donkey rides, brass bands,
But I know what I will see,
Little girls with blue eyes and long blonde hair.

Ankle socks flashing and bright summer shoes,
Ribbons and bobbles and gay coloured clothes,
Shining eyes, high voices, excited chatter,
Smiling up into their mothers' faces,
I ache to see my little girl's smile again.

Just for a moment I catch a glance of a girl
Who has a way or a look that I know so well,
My heart leaps, then thuds to stop,
It cannot be her . . . you fool!
Buying two ice-creams instead of three,
Two tickets for the zoo, not three,
The car has more room,
Less squabbles
So hateful the gap.

It all seems so strange without her there,
We wander, aimless, through the bank holiday crowds,
But always searching, searching for that familiar face,
Of our little girl with blue eyes and long blonde hair.

Marilyn Shawe

TO TONY

So many things have happened since you went away,
I've thought about so many things that I would like to say,
If I could have you here with me, if only for a day.

I know you cannot hear me, though I still talk to you,
If only you could answer me the way you used to do.
We'd talk about the happy days, and perhaps the sad ones too.

I never thought I'd lose you, life seemed so ideal,
Suddenly it's shattered, nothing seems quite real,
I wish that I could tell you the way I really feel.

Janet Dickinson

PART TWO

SHARING THE LOSS

A bereaved family's greatest need is to have friends who are prepared to stay alongside, not only through the tears but through the anger and accusations, the guilt and denial and all the naked, inexpressable grief. With nothing wise to say all one can do is to stand by and, simply by sharing the grief, help to dissipate it a little. This is part of the task of friends – to help keep the memory of loved ones alive, to show concern for one another.

David Dodman

Bereaved parents want to be a normal part of society. They don't want to burden everyone else with their pain, but the grief must be allowed the opportunity and time to work itself out. Bereaved parents also need the chance to talk about their dead children, and the opportunity to say their names. Bereaved parents may have buried their children but they are not burying their memories, and neither should they ... there is one thing worse than speaking ill of the dead – and that is not speaking of them at all.

Jo Edwards

WHY?

A POEM BY A LITTLE GIRL
ABOUT HER FRIEND WHO DIED

I thought we'd grow up
    Together
I thought we'd go out
    Together
I thought we'd be friends
    For ever
    But no!
It's not fair!
    Oh Clare!

Michelle Garvey

WHY?

Why take the precious and leave the worthless?
Why take the doers of good and leave the thoughtless?
Why take the hearts of gold and leave the soulless?
Why take the light and leave only the darkness?

John Gosney

WHY COULDN'T YOU STAY?

I didn't hear you cry
I didn't hear you moan
But quietly in your sleep you died
Leaving me alone.

I loved you very much
What did I do wrong?
I nurtured you with love
You were so big and strong.

31

I miss your tears and laughter
And your happy smiling face
My heart is numb and heavy
No one can take your place.

I wonder why you left us
That sad November day,
You were my love and hope
Why couldn't you stay?

Heather Parry

TO MY SON TONY

Outside I look quite happy
But inside myself I cry,
So young, so brave, so loving,
Why did you have to die?

I remember all the good times
Those happy carefree days,
You showed such love and kindness
In so many, many ways.

I loved and wanted you so much
My gentle, thoughtful boy,
The years we spent together
You brought me so much joy.

Perhaps, someday, I'll thank the Lord
For all those happy years,
Perhaps someday I'll think of you
And not shed any tears.

Till then, my son, you're in my thoughts
My heart is filled with pain,
Dear Lord, please keep him safely
Until we meet again.

Janet Dickinson

32

QUESTIONS

Why do children have to die
Why does it happen to children
Why did you go away my only one
Why are we left with this pain?

  'Never to see or touch or hold
  Never to watch you grow up
  Never to care for you
  Never to scold
  Never no more to see or hold.'

What is the point of bearing this pain
What is the meaning of grieving
What is the reason for suffering so
What is the purpose in living?

  'Never to see or touch or hold
  Never to watch you grow up
  Never to care for you
  Never to scold
  Never no more to see or hold.'

Give me a reason
Give me a plan
Give me a path I can follow
Give me the strength to carry on
Give me a purpose in being.

  'Never to see or touch or hold
  Never to watch you grow up
  Never to care for you
  Never to scold
  Never no more to see or hold.'

Are you watching my life's struggle
Are you waiting there for me
Are you sad when I am sad
Are you wishing me not to be?

'Never to see or touch or hold
Never to watch you grow up
Never to care for you
Never to scold
Never no more to see or hold.'

I will never know all the answers
To this pain I have to bear
But in searching for these answers
I have found much comfort there.

I have seen and touched and held you
I have watched you grow
I have given birth to you
I have loved and cared for you
I will always love you so.

I am grateful for your life
I am proud to call you son
I am thankful for the love and joy you showed me
– that is mine for always.

Jo Edwards

DAVID

My little brother loved football
You couldn't keep him away
He loved his football oh so much
It took his life away.

He only fell upon the grass
The soft slushy ground
But it was that soft and slushy grass
That stopped his heart go pound.

Why did you have to leave us?
You've made us all so sad
I know you wouldn't want that
But now I feel so bad.

I'd shouted at you sharply
Also your football
For breaking a few flowers
I wish I'd not at all.

Please forgive me David
For not saying goodbye
You see my heart was broken
I heard it crack inside.

My little baby brother
Lying unconscious
I prayed that you would waken
I did make such a fuss.

I'm glad you went with no pain
And playing your football
I'll miss you kicking in the drive
But I'll miss you most of all.

Jen Prescott

Jen, aged fourteen, wrote this poem on Easter Sunday, hours after David had died suddenly while playing football in the family garden. Although David was nine years old, doctors believe that he died from a form of Cot Death Syndrome.

TEDDY

My aching breast, my broken heart.
The flowing milk, in this empty dark.
Child of my womb, breath of my breath.
I'll mourn forever, your lonely death.

You gave me life, I learnt to love.
My *Teddy*, my darling, my angel above.
Out of sorrow they say will come joy.
I'll never forget you, my baby boy.

35

Why did you leave me, why did you die?
I say in the night, as I wait for your cry.

I think of things that we would have done.
Sleep now for ever, my darling, my son.

Emily Rothwell

In memory of Edward Ian Rothwell 12.11.89–19.1.90, 11 weeks 1 day.

A FATHER'S LAMENT

Scraps of paper
Hoarded for years
Messages scrawled
Just fill me with tears
To look at them now
It makes me so sad
For most of them say
I love you Dad.

Holiday snaps
Of our visit to Spain
Just serve to remind
Of the loss and the pain
The smile on her lips
The gleam in her eye
Tell me O Lord
Why she had to die.

Allan Brigden

WHY?

Why were our children taken?
Are we the unfortunate few?
They were our reason for living,
Whom we pass on our future to.

Did someone decree we were chosen?
As able to suffer the pain?
To travel the pathway of life
Not seeing our children again?

Where is the sense and the reason
For God to do such a deed?
To deprive us of part of our being,
The life that was born of a seed.

We are not special people,
We hurt, and we bleed, and we cry.
We're as normal as you and the next one,
So, can somebody tell me why?

Anne Alexander

SHARING

ECHOES OF GRIEF

I hear the echoes of my own lament
   In your new born grief,
I see the shadow of my deep dark pain
   In your bewildered eyes,
I feel the sickening wrench of separation
   In your bleak face of despair.

I know the old fierce fervour of longing for my child
   In your aching empty arms,
I remember my fruitless search for reason
   In your heartwrung 'Why God, why?'
I too was numbed by the unfairness of life
   As in your shocked disbelief.

I recognise the shattering of faith, hope, reason
   In your stooping shoulders,
I understand the hopeless helplessness that was me.
   I speak your language.

Marilyn Shawe

JUST BE THERE

I only want you to be there
To listen, to understand, to share.
To accept my sadness and show me that you care,
And give me the freedom to cry out with despair.
Please don't try to change the way I feel,
Or take my grief away,
It is the only feeling I have left.

Marilyn Shawe

HELP

Do not turn away from my grief,
It will not harm you,
But do not ask me to turn away from my grief,
If I turn away from my grief,
It may well harm me.

Do not ignore me, or my pain,
Both are real to me.
Acknowledgement is what I seek,
And time and space for me to heal.

Do not cross the road as I approach,
Do not add to my burden,
My suffering is not contagious,
Nor would I want it to be.

Do not pretend nothing has happened
To try and ease my pain,
Do not be afraid, or apprehensive,
To use my dead child's name.

I do not wait on you to lay
The burden that I carry,
But you can ease my path ahead.
Just stay behind me as I tread
This uphill battle to go on,
To mend my broken life, to start anew
Without the one who inside me grew.

Jo Edwards

A SHOCKING DAY

'Oh, this weather, isn't it a shocking day? It's never stopped raining all morning, and to think I've had my washing hung out since yesterday. I can't bring it in because it's absolutely soaking. I'll never catch up with my ironing this week.' I really do not understand what Edna is flapping about, nobody died of wet laundry.

In my secret world I relish the wildness of the wind, and the driving rain has a ferocious rage about it which matches my own violent emotions, and the grey clouds are no darker than my heart.

Edna perseveres ... How inconsiderate of her daughters to expect clean clothes every day, and her with the weather to contend with.

Reinforcements arrive in the baggy shapes of Peggy and Mary, windswept and frowning, and battling against the elements. Peggy's indignant expression foretells ominous signs of disgruntlement. 'My daughter is driving me mad. She's got so fussy about her food. Won't eat anything but health food. All this expensive stuff. Ridiculous it is. I told her while she's under our roof she eats what we do, egg and chips never did no one any harm. I shall be glad when she leaves home and has to look after herself. She'll see then.' There is a general clucking of agreement.

My thoughts start to drift away to far places in my mind. To a place where real problems and anguish are the order of the day. A white antiseptic awesome place that breathes terror into the hearts of many souls. A place where many parents would go down on their hands and knees if there was the faintest hope that they would ever see their child eat anything ever again. To a place where hopes are few and disappointments are many and heartbreaking. To a little girl's eyes pleading silently for release from pain, where a little hand clutches mine trustingly.

Mary's voice drones on in the unreal reality of the present. 'I think this lipstick is the wrong shade for me. Uncle Wilf died last night, eighty-nine he was. Died in his sleep terrible shock it was. Does this one suit me – passionate peach? I don't think Auntie Maggy is ever going to get over it. We're all devastated. No, I think I'll plump for the frosted pink.' Everyone nods in approval at her choice of cosmetics.

I can see a young face in my memory, of a girl on the threshold of being a teenager, whose skin is as soft as velvet and who has a smile which no make up could enhance, and a sparkle in her eyes that no false colouring could do justice to. The face is contorted in agony now, the eyes inward and long-suffering. The smile is a struggle. Her whole existence is a struggle, survival is a losing battle. She upholds me with the power of her love, her courage lends us both dignity in the degrading throes of dying. The glow that always surrounds her and encapsulates all those who are near with love, surrounds her still, even in the cruel hand of death.

I hear myself gasping to the receding backs of the women, 'My daughter is dead. I had to watch her die. Why doesn't anyone talk to me about it, ask me how I am, listen to me? It is so hard to carry on, every day is a battle just to exist. Help me.'

Silence. Downcast eyes. Sidelong glances. Nervous coughing. Suddenly I am on my own.

Marilyn Shawe

TO FRIENDS AT THE ALDER CENTRE
ON MAKING A PROGRAMME

It hasn't been easy, hearing your grief.
I have felt your pain, and made it my own.
Tears have come easily, as I listened to your loss.
Tears for your children, so much loved.
So much missed.

It hasn't been easy, to be part of your 'crowd',
To be a small part of your insignificant day.
A tiny hiccup of talk in your endless empty time.
Someone to reach to and touch for a moment.

I have felt that I ought to be guilty,
Imposing a film on your grief and longing,
Structuring pictures of your private selves.
But I have not been guilty, or for that matter structuring,
Merely listening, and feeling your hurt.

Few pictures come to mind but your laughter and warmth.
You have made me welcome in your dark places,
Invited me in to share, and be healed.
With no loss of my own I have imagined the worst –
My children dead.

41

It has not been easy, but living isn't.
You live that all the time, and I for a moment.
Thank you.

Nikki Cheetam

MY THOUGHTS AS A HELPER

Before I go any further, may I say that I only want to help in any small way I can? I offer no comfort or platitudes, just my thoughts as a helper and onlooker to you all. My involvement with the Centre came as a result of our experience on C3, the oncology ward in Alder Hey Children's Hospital, when our youngest child, Emma, was having treatment for malignant cancer. In the words of a lovely bereaved parent, 'How wonderful to meet a parent whose child survived.'

Yes, we do have our daughter after a year of chemotherapy and an operation which several times put her life very much at risk, making us face the possibility which for you all became reality. We both feel very strongly the threat of relapse, and worse, hanging over our little girl's head, but one of our biggest comforts is seeing you all soldier on despite your lives being irrevocably shattered. Not only do you soldier on, but you find courage to help others in the same position. How often must you be confronted by a similar situation or painful reminder of your own grief, whilst helping another desolate parent.

Sheila Chorley

THE VISITOR

My friend, you may visit me from time to time and I will come close to the edge of my desolate territory, to catch a glimpse of what we once shared. You could even touch my hand some days, through the holes in the fencing, but you would feel nothing. As my substance has seeped out and strayed elsewhere. You are right when you say I have gone through a door that you cannot enter: a 'one way only' door. I am forever searching the universe for a warm glow that my child is near, that his path has just crossed

42

mine and his fragrance and laughter are still around, if I really strain my senses. My heart is leaping to pour the love over him that is accumulating without release . . .

You are brave, my friend for risking coming so near – very few do. Some stand at a distance and think they can help by inviting me out for some happy company. How shallow and sad that they succeed only in erecting another fence. If they had only once spoken his name, and really cared, instead of trying to wipe him out. But no.

You must sense that you risk rejection some days, when you call me over, because there is only one face that I am longing to see, and only one hand reaching out. Other days I feel concern for you that you come so close and might not be able to find your way back to the outside world. But don't worry, if the time ever comes for you to pass through the 'one way gate' you are never alone, because Jesus surrounds you constantly. Little things that you would normally take for granted become treasures beyond treasure. He seems to say, 'Tarry a little while at this half way mark and you can share yourself between what is to come and what you are leaving.' There is no fear in this place and no time, no darkness and no brightness. People are not solid – you seem to walk through each other, instead of going around. In fact it is more a case of gliding than walking. There are no homes or furniture. As you never stop to rest, you don't get tired. A few moments at the fence from time to time, then off again, in total submission, to let God have his will, whatever that may be. So long as he unites us, a complete family again, in heaven, it will all have been worth while.

Thanks for visiting.

Maureen Prescott

LETTING GO

JUST ONE DAY

I often think how happy I would be
To have just one day a year with you
And we could do those same old things
The way we used to do.
But then this could never be I know,
For I could never let you go.

John Gosney

THE CHILD WE GREW

A thousand nights
A thousand days
Are bitter pills
Time can't erase.
The child we grew
Within us two
Will never know our golden days.
She'll never walk
Or laugh or run
Into a field with
A setting sun.

Dot Ellis

LETTING GO

When I saw Amanda lying there wired up to the tubes and wires of the life support machine, I knew that she had already gone from here. Part of me could not comprehend the fact that this inert body was my lovely loving daughter, who only a few hours ago had been so full of fun and life and laughter. They told me she was brain dead.

I didn't know what dead meant then. She was breathing, she was warm, but she wasn't there. The sane reasoning part of me said, 'You have to let her go, set her free from this poor sick body.' The crazily fierce, all protective, all powerful maternal instinct in me said, 'I'll never let her go, she's my baby, she needs me, I need her.' I did not know how to let her go, but I knew I must.

How do you say 'Yes' to turning off your child's life support? How do you persuade yourself that they will never return to you as they were before, when you can see them lying there so vulnerable, looking as if they were only asleep for a little while? When any moment you expect their eyelids to flicker open and recognition to bring a smile to their lips, and their arms to wind tightly round your neck because they are so relieved to find you there in this strange and frightening place called hospital.

All the past times when she had recovered from bouts of severe life-threatening illness flashed through my mind. She had come through worse than this before. Always smiling, nothing could hold her down for long. She always had the strength to sustain the both of us.

It was her strength then that was to pull me through this time. Letting go of her was the hardest thing I've ever had to do. But I loved her so much, I couldn't hold her back. It was the only thing I could do for her. So while she lay unconscious I told her all the things I wanted her to know, that I loved her, that I wanted desperately to make her well again, to try and open her eyes for me, but if she couldn't, if it was too hard, not to be frightened, not to be sad, I would always keep her safe in my heart, just go and be happy darling.

'Just go and be happy darling.'

Marilyn Shawe

TAKING CARE

Who's taking care of you now?
Who makes sure you're wrapped up against the cold?
Who tries to cheer you up when you are down?
I've worried about these things.

You are my responsibility.
The best job I'll ever have.
But I don't have to worry about you any more.
You are safe now, from any further harm.
I'd give the world to have those worries back.
But I can't have them.
You are as bright as a button.
And I love you.
But I don't need to worry any more.

John Gosney

ANOTHER YEAR

Another Christmas without you, son.
Another, and your birthday will soon be here.
Another year without you, Stephen.
Another year just knowing you are not here.
Another year, son, without your smiling face and silly little jokes.
Another year without my gentle giant.
Another year without your footsteps on my path.
Another year I just can't bear to face.
Another year of tears I still shed.
Another year that I have to struggle through.
Another year that I might make it through.
Another year that I might see you.
Another year. Please try and help me through.
Another year, son, I don't think I can take.

Love from Mum.

Margaret Moyle

PRECIOUS MEMORIES

IN MEMORY OF CHRISTINE ELLIS

When I think about Chris I remember her smile
and the way it lit up her whole face
and the sound of her voice, slightly husky,
as she played with the kids at my place.
With her wickedly dry sense of humour
she inherited no doubt from her Mum
and the way she tried to join in all the games
and be part of the general fun.

When I think about Chris I remember her laugh
as the children all played here together
running around in the garden.
That's how she'll stay in my memory for ever.
I remember her eyes bright with laughter
though sometimes there must have been tears
but it's the happiness that I remember
when I look back in my mind on those years.

Norah Cottignies

THE BEST PRESENT

I remember the last gift you ever bought for me. It was when you
were eleven years old and you were helping at the Girl Guides'
Christmas Fair. I had only just arrived at the church hall, which
by now was heaving with people. Through the crowds I saw your
beaming little face, which was flushed and happy from the exer-
tion of serving the rush of Christmas shoppers who were anxious
to get bargains at your stall.

When you saw me struggling through the throng you gave me
a radiant smile, which held your special brand of inner glow, and
outshone the brightness of all the Christmassy glitter in the hall.
It gave me a rush of tender pride to know that you could still

smile like that even when life was dealing you a rough time with your poor health.

As I drew near I could see you were bursting to tell me something. You looked so happy as you told me that you had managed to do all your Christmas shopping at the Fair before it had been opened to the public. A gold chain for Grandma, a scarf for Grandad, a mug for Dad, perfume for your sister and a huge drum kit for your brother!

'They only wanted 50p for it on the toy counter Mum', you exclaimed jubilantly. I thought grimly how much I would pay to return it. Then you added mysteriously that you had a special present for me which I was not to see.

Tired and happy you met me at the door when all had finished. I can still picture us now pushing our bicycles home on that dismal December afternoon, you were loaded down with carrier bags and rolls of wrapping paper, which you assured me you could manage on your own. In your usual efficient, capable way you soon had all your gifts wrapped and accompanied by home-made loving little cards placed under the Christmas tree. I still had no idea what you had bought me.

On Christmas day you watched anxiously as I opened your present. It was a torch, but not an ordinary torch, it had a siren on it! 'It's in case you ever get attacked or mugged when you're out, Mum', you said kindly. You had even bought batteries for it. I put them in and turned it on. The light worked but the siren was mute.

The disappointment and embarrassment in your eyes was acute. But I was so thrilled to think that you cared about my safety and well being to try and protect me in your small way. I still have it today, Amanda, although you are gone. It still doesn't work but it symbolises the most precious gift I ever had, the most precious gift of all, the gift of your wonderful love for me.

Marilyn Shawe

DYING TO DIE

Our daughter Katie died on 16 April 1982 (the Friday after Easter) aged eight years. She had had leukaemia for three years.

I would like to tell you about her message on the day she died. It helped John and me, especially when we went through the questioning times of 'Is there a God', 'Is there life after death', which I am sure all bereaved parents must ask.

Katie was surrounded by love, and prayers were being said by people all over the country that she might be cured. On the Friday she died, I prayed that if God was going to take her, please let her give me some sign that there is something more than this earthly life. I have always believed in God and heaven, but I knew that I would always question, and I had heard about other children who had given messages.

We were able to look after Katie at home, with the help of our GP and community nurses. She was only in the bed for the last two days. At 2.30 p.m. on Friday, Katie had just had an injection, and we were sitting round the bed talking to the doctor. Katie suddenly sat up, outstretched her arms and shouted, 'I'm dying.' I said, 'What to go to the loo?' Katie shouted, 'No, I'm dying.' She flung her arms so tight around my neck and said, 'Oh Mummy, I'm dying to die, I'm dying to die', over and over again. Then she said, 'Is my heart still beating.' 'Yes', I said. She replied, 'Well stop it, Mummy.'

I laid her down and told her to go into a nice sleep, and she went to sleep. At 5.00 p.m. she awoke and wanted to walk to the toilet (much to the amazement of the nurse). She walked back to the bedroom, sat on the chair, and ordered the nurse, John and myself to change the sheets on the bed. She then went into a deep sleep, and died two hours later.

Katie was a very feminine little girl, who loved dressing up, and I believe she was dressing up for a party. She was happy at the end, and was 'dying to die'.

Katie had not been told she was going to die, but she surprised us when in the last two weeks she changed her prayers from 'please make me healthy and strong and better again' to 'please look after Mummy, Daddy and Andrew (her brother)'. Also she insisted on going to school right up to the Easter holidays, even though she was tired, because she wanted to finish making us an Easter card, on which she had added the words 'I love you, Mummy and Daddy' (the only child in the class to add this). The card is now framed and on our bedroom wall.

I believe these children that are taken from us so young are very special. Katie gave us so much love in her short life, and was always happy, despite having to suffer awful treatment and losing her hair, etc.

It is now seven years since Katie died, and never a day goes by where we do not think of her, with lots of love.

Time does heal (I used to hate that saying). We can enjoy life again, and when you have been through hell you appreciate happiness, and I know Katie would rather us be happy. She hated it when we were upset.

Also I know that what she saw that day must be a wonderful place, and I hope and pray that one day we will be with her again for eternity.

Doreen and John Gillam

MY COMPANIONS

I wake them up and dust them down, my companions every day,
They are all I have to cling to as I struggle on my way,
So precious, are they to me, their value cannot be measured,
My old worn-out memories for ever will be treasured.

John Gosney

HOLDING ON

꧁꧂

TAKE HEART, YOUR CHILD IS SAFE

'I am telling the truth; whoever hears my words and believes in him who sent me, has eternal life. He will not be judged, but has already passed from death to life. I am telling you the truth: the time is coming – the time has already come – when the dead will hear the voice of the son of God, and those who hear it will come to life' (John 5:24–5).

God speaks to us through his word – the Bible. Before David died (thirteen months ago), turning to the Bible was something I always pushed off till I'd done something else. Needless to say my Bible rarely got opened. Now it has come alive for me, as it is my main link with David. I am still not the type of reader that my Christian friends are, and I cannot concentrate for very long. However, over the months, I have coloured over many verses (mostly in the New Testament) with different coloured pencils. These are verses that shout out with hope and comfort, and enable me to face the day ahead. Sometimes even to face the next five minutes seems an impossible task. However, I am finding that Jesus comes that much closer when I'm at my most distressed. The first few months he always provided someone at the door or 'phone to help me through. Now I know he expects me to turn to him. He's the only one who understands just how much pain we carry inside us. Realisation has dawned that no one in the world can really help – they can only walk short stretches of our lonely road of suffering with us. My faith has grown a lot, as I find closeness to the Lord means closeness to David also.

I no longer want to be an intellectual Christian as I thought I needed to be, before David's death. Jesus said, 'I assure you that unless you change and become like children, you will never enter the kingdom of heaven.' How much more helpless could anyone be, than after losing their child? We are just heartbroken children ourselves, and our heavenly Father is the only one who can make things bearable. But we have to ask him to come in and help us. He's waiting eagerly to do so. At my blackest moments, I never doubt that God is to be trusted. He loves our children far more than we ourselves do. We may not understand why our world has been shattered but we can come to accept that all is under control and our children are totally safe. It is exciting knowing that we are getting closer to seeing them again with every passing day.

We can now begin to taste Christ's suffering as he gave his life for us. Did we have any idea what real suffering was, before entering this terrible grief? Now we can identify with all who suffer in any way, and understanding that for much of the earth's population, suffering is a way of life. How blind we were!

Maureen Prescott

MY ANCHOR

For some months now I have been upset by advice given to me. 'All things change', I was told, and shouldn't I go forward and grow as a person. These statements made me unhappy because to go forward is to leave something behind.

I have been struggling with these thoughts for some time, and I have finally managed to sort the situation out, regarding myself.

I am aware that things will change; I have very little control over most aspects of life. The idea that I have come up with is perfect for me; it allows for change, but gives stability as well.

I imagine that my grief, my loss of my beloved Clare, is an anchor to which I am attached by a long chain. I can move around my anchor to allow for change, but wherever I am I will always be close to my anchor.

This idea has helped me to get my emotions into some sort of order.

John Gosney

GUILTY OR NOT GUILTY?

When we lose a parent, however much it hurts, we accept the inevitability and the natural justice of our parents predeceasing us, take up the baton and carry on with our lives.

When we lose a child we cannot grasp this reversal of the

natural laws. It contradicts our instinctive logic and leaves us floundering in a frantic search for reasons. Being frail and fallible we accept too soon that it is a punishment without looking for a crime. The knowledge that our lost child is innocent while we have made mistakes adds to the guilt of the survivor. We fuel our remorse by remembering only our omissions and forget the everyday ways by which our child was reassured of our love.

If we persist in punishing ourselves and paying a penance we could never deserve, counting the loss but ignoring the value of what we still have, we risk losing everything. We must decide who we are crying for: our child or ourselves. If the answer is hard to face, we are in danger of debasing our child's contribution to our lives. It could be a destructive force instead of a brief but priceless blessing.

Charles O'Hara

WITHOUT ANY FEAR

From the depths of despair to lights untold
Through many a turmoil passed,
Many the time it was as before,
But now is as now at last.

In the beginning the despair was brought
Through things that just happened in life
Not through they is, or they are, or they ought,
Nor through any fault of my wife.

My love was taken in her tender years
To a life beyond the vale,
That's when it started to hurt me, the fears,
So I tried to drown them in ale.

For years I was drunk and in a sorry state,
That would not do credit to me,
Then alas I knew not what was my fate,
My eyes opened, and now I can see.

From the drink and the anguish of all I had done,
From the things of what people say,
To the raptures of life, to having fun,
To living just for today.

Today is the greatest, for life is good,
'Tis as good as the one I stand near,
For living one day at a time as I should
I live without any fear.

Trevor Maude

THEY STILL CONTINUE TO BE

Why do we weep for our children
Who have passed on sooner than we?
They have only moved into the next room,
And they still continue to be.

Why do we feel bitter towards God,
And ask 'Why did this happen to me?'
The whys and the wherefores don't matter
For our children continue to be.

We feel angry and frightened and lonely
And through tears unable to see
Life in its fullness and wonder
As our children continue to be.

We have all had these feelings at some time
I am sure that you all will agree
But our love for them goes on for ever
As they still continue to be.

I can honestly say that I thank God
For the loan of my son, Paul, to me
And I hold in my heart lovely memories
And I know he continues to be.

If we open our hearts to our children
And know that they want us to see
Their happiness, pleasure and sunshine
Where they still continue to be.

Rose Foster

AT ONE WITH NATURE

I feel at one with the grey clouds rushing across the sky.
I find solace in the loneliness of the high places.
I am at ease on the rainswept, windy headland.
I get comfort from the storm.
I am at one with nature.
But only when she is as unsettled as I am.

John Gosney

LIFE GOES ON

THE TWO OF ME

The two of me lives life side by side
One of me is public the other I hide,
When you see me with my everyday face
It appears quite normal, quite commonplace,
But you wouldn't know it's an artful act
The other me is broken and that's a fact.

Life still goes on, it has to be
We're compelled to plod on through adversity,
We weather the storms and brave the rain
We stumble along even through great pain.

Each day one of me tries to go on living
To do normal things and be loving and giving,
The other me shrinks like a shrivelled flower
Feeling more bitter and hurt by each passing hour.

The innermost me is shrouded in grief
Locked in its power there is no relief,
The two of me looks to the future ahead
One of me with hope, the other with dread.

Marilyn Shawe

THOUGHTS OVER CHRISTMAS

These thoughts came to me over Christmas when so many, now
painful reminders of happier days resurfaced as I was taking down
the Christmas cards and arranging to send them to charities.

If, like me, other parents saved the birth congratulation cards
with thoughts of sharing the contents with their children when
they had grown into adulthood, and saved 'get well' cards (if
appropriate) when their children were ill, what can be more

harrowing than the cards of condolence received on the death of your child?

Sometimes these cards can bring comfort to the bereaved if the deceased person has lived a full, long and healthy life. The sentiments can help in the coming to terms with the loss of that person, but how incongruous it is to associate condolence cards with children.

Unlike the birth and get well cards, I felt unable to display the condolence cards when my daughter, Kirstie Jane, died eight years ago, aged ten. I was at a loss as to what to do with them. They gave me no comfort, but only served to reinforce the horror of the situation. Those who sent them did so with good intentions which I appreciated, but each one I received felt like a knife in my heart.

All of these cards now have a place, out of sight in a safe place. I know their location but am unable to read them again while at the same time am unable to part with them.

Anne Alexander

TIME'S EVIL WORK

Tears don't flow so freely now,
Time's evil work goes on,
Its fog drifts through my senses,
Real life has gone,
Robbed of the intensity,
It's stealing from me still.
Time couldn't cure my heartache,
So my memory it chose to kill.

John Gosney

TWO YEARS ON

A quiet time to listen only to my thoughts. Everybody needs a quiet time to listen to the silence that is within us all; to catch the rain in our hands; to catch a snowflake and watch it melt with the heat of your body that tells you you *are* alive. Yes, alive and part of this world even when you feel you are only existing. A part, yet apart. Surely we each must have a part to play in this unfolding saga we call 'living'.

I listened to a man say that everything is either before his son died, or after. His son's death has become the focal point of his living.

And so it is with me. I had not realised. My life before David seems meaningless. It is a strange thought that meaning to life has come from death. I remember rationally talking to myself shortly after David had died and saying 'OK – David has gone – my life is over – pain, anguish, despair will fill the rest of my days – happiness has gone for me, existence is my lot in a world I cannot see, a world that is just grey, nothing, a world where the sun does not shine, the birds do not sing, the seasons are one and the same – no promise for the future, no hope, no dreams – just nothing.'

I faced that thought and, having decided that suicide was not the answer, I looked at whatever was left to me, gritted my teeth and went forth into battle to endure the remainder of my life.

Now I have taken a quiet time out – not to do anything – time for me, time for my thoughts to roam, time to mourn.

When I looked at my future, I saw two paths, two ways I felt I could go. One was to launch myself into the abyss of pain which had opened up for me, to savour it, nurture it even, because that pain was David, it was my only link. I wanted to shut myself up in a black box with David, my pain, my reality, my life. I wanted to embrace it, hide in it, until ultimately I would die in it.

The other path was one which led to the world, to go out and shout, I am in pain, I am here, I am alive, I don't want to be but I am. I am not going to waste this life I have been given, I will not throw it away on a funeral pyre, I will not tarnish David's memory by wasting it, I will not waste David's life by wasting my own. David came to me and he went but I will not let his going be a negative influence on the life I have. Everything has a purpose, for every negative there is a positive, for every cause there is an effect. It is up to us to choose.

And now it is two years, two months and four days since David died. I remember so clearly making that decision. It has been the longest two years of my life. I have experienced so many emotions.

58

The one thing that stands out is the fact that grief is not just about pain – it is damned hard work. Just keeping on your feet. I feel as if I am trudging up an enormous sandhill with two heavy suitcases. Sometimes I cannot look sideways, or up ahead, I can only look to the next half step or just standing still, keeping my balance, trying not to fall sideways or backwards. I think I have reached the stage where I don't fall backwards any more – I can just about keep my balance now and sometimes my balance is such that I can afford a sideways glance, and on good days I can even afford to look ahead to the next couple of steps.

One day I will be able to stand up straight, open my eyes wide and look into the horizon where the sun sets – but remembering also that the sun rises.

Jo Edwards

DAVID

Life goes on in my little home
And the days, somehow, go by,
A thousand memories stir my heart,
And I know, somehow, I'll cry.

But love peeps through my window pane
And wakes within my mind
The happiness of days gone by
The joys I left behind.

The son I loved would never wish
Me drowned in endless pain
So I must weave threads
Of life into pattern once again.

So . . . David, for you I'll open doors
And let your 'sun' shine in,
The love you 'send me', darling son,
May make my life begin.

Barbara Simon

59

ONLY TEMPORARY?

In the morning I get up and there is nothing to do.
I tell myself it's only temporary.

In the afternoon I am bored, I dislike what I am.
I tell myself it's only temporary.

At night alone I listen to my heart beating.
I tell myself it's only temporary.

Dot Ellis

SCREAM!

At birth, scream we must,
And scream we do, otherwise we're dead.
Through life scream, we must,
Through all our pain.
If scream we don't,
We die inside instead.

Convention dictates. It states:
'No, I'm sorry, there is no wailing wall here,
You will just have to . . .
Hold your breath.'

But this woman defies convention,
And she comes through screaming,
And starts her life again.

Jill Jones

PART THREE

LOVING OUR CHILDREN

Some parents are deeply hurt when outsiders say, 'But you still have other children don't you?' Other children may be a consolation but not a substitute. Don't offer extreme advice, such as have another baby to replace the missing one. Avoid saying 'I know how you feel'. The truth of the matter is that no one knows what another person is going through. It takes someone who has lost a child to know what losing a child really means. Another approach that can be disturbing is the condescending one that assures the bereaved 'Time is a great healer' or the question 'Have you got over it yet?' That seems to us to mean forgetting our child and we never want to, nor ever shall do that.

David Dodman

LOVING IS FOR EVER

FOR BABY ANDREW

Together we will walk
Together hand in hand
My son and me,
To look at life's pleasures
With little eyes,
Look to one another
And to be sure
Of a Mother's love
For her new born
    Son.

A little extra sleep
A little more slumber
A little folding the hands
    To rest.

    Hope,
What have we got other than hope?
    For without hope
    There is nothing.

Sue Clarke

FOR DODY

There's still so much I miss about not seeing you any more –
The whisper soft touch of your fingers
Your loving, soggy kiss.
A giggle, more like an explosion
Of tiny droplets of love,
The way you clapped your tiny hands,
The mischief made by 'pokey' finger,
The look which said 'Life's grand!'

The love we shared was pure as you
And is still as strong today
And when the sky breaks into sunshine
I feel your love shine through,
But even on the dark days,
When I'm sunk in deep despair
I know my darling Dody
Our love is always there.

Ceri Maddocks

David had Down's Syndrome and died aged fifteen months from leukaemia. He died at home, in my arms, where he belonged, and although our home is now 200 miles away, his spirit is still with us, where it belongs.

AN EMPTY KNEE

Tom loved to sit with me at night.
We'd watch each other's eyes,
Exchanging mental thoughts of love
And strokes for baby sighs.

We learned each other's faces
As we talked without a word,
No one else could hear us
When we said how much we cared.

I loved to sit with Tom at night.
I'd watch him watching me,
We'd make each other happy
While Tom sat there on my knee.

I miss him now that he's not there.
No gurgles of delight,
When I'm sitting in our cosy chair
With an empty knee at night.

Dave Sutton

A SPECIAL LITTLE BOY

Tom joined our family on 1 May 1986. From the moment he was born, both Dave and I, and other members of our family, felt that Tom was a very special little boy. We didn't love him any more or less than his elder brothers, but we felt that somehow Tom was different.

As soon as Tom arrived in the delivery room at Mill Road Hospital and I held him in my arms, he gazed up at me and I felt a shiver run through my body. I find it hard to explain the feelings I had, but I know that one of them was fear – fear of what, I didn't know.

That night in hospital I dreamt that Tom had died of a cot death. I woke up and Tom wasn't by my bed. I ran to the nursery and picked him up and held him tightly.

When Tom came home the feelings of uneasiness gradually lessened, but there was always something at the back of my mind. If it ever surfaced it was pushed right back again. Tom was everything you could ever wish for in a baby. He was bonny and bright, he slept well and smiled at everyone. I was so proud of our three lovely boys.

Dave spoilt him rotten. I would come home from work at 10 p.m. at night (after putting Tom to bed at 6.30) and Tom would be sitting on Dave's lap giggling and talking away. I would ask Dave, 'What is Tom doing up?', and Dave would sheepishly reply, 'Oh I just woke him up for a chat' – I'm so glad he did now.

We found Tom dead in his cot on 19 December 1986. I still find it hard to believe and accept. I still ask, 'Why?' He was, and still is, so very special. I am so glad I was his mother.

We now have another addition to our family – Katie. Katie is sixteen months old and it hasn't been an easy sixteen months. I wake up every morning with a knot of fear in my stomach until I hear her, and then I relax. Katie will be the only one never to have met Tom, but she will know that she had three older brothers not two.

Whenever we are together as a family, we will always be incomplete – one of us is missing. My dearest wish would have been to see my four children together.

Sue Sutton

ODE TO A DAUGHTER

So fair my lovely, our daughter,
You danced across our lives,
But life has only one chapter,
Further reading lies in our minds.

Reflecting on nature's progression,
It is nobody's fault nor design
That such is not a transgression,
Nor intervention divine.

Assailed on all sides by remembrance,
Seeing matters both trivial and small,
It is because love surrounds us
That we have survived at all.

'Tis not the length of the chapter,
Nor a glorification that palls,
'Tis the knowledge of what lies hereafter,
There's life after death after all.

The waxing and waning of healing
Lies within us all.
There is no use in appealing
To Nature nor Life, one and all.

After this cheerless beginning
We often look back and review
The laughter, the love, the healing,
Brought on by the gift we'd renew.

Reflecting is part of the process,
A prelude to letting go,
Because you see she's within us
For ever and ever anon.

Joe Waring

ROBBIE'S SONG

Days gone by was a time,
When there was a child so fine.
I loved him, he loved me,
He loved everything he'd see.
It takes time only time,
   It takes time.

He would run how he'd go,
How things worked out he'd want to know.
A lifetime's fun, a lifetime's fears,
He packed into thirteen years.
It takes time only time,
   It takes time.

This son of mine became my friend,
I never thought these days would end.
Days gone by I wonder when,
Perhaps sometime I'll smile again.
   It takes time.

Ian MacLeod

THE BOND OF LOVE

It's hard to understand, how I could know Clare would not survive her operation. Although by nature I am a pessimist, it had nothing to do with pessimism. I felt it as a certainty, that it could not be altered, that it was fate. I was as sure of this, as you are that tomorrow will follow today.

The bond of love that I have for Clare, I liken to a taut thread that ran between us. When the thread was disturbed at Clare's end, I would feel a disturbance at mine. This is the only way to describe how on many occasions I would have a feeling about Clare that proved to be correct. It was a stronger reality than intuition.

To see Clare at Christmas time opening her presents and going to parties, saying that this was her best Christmas, was so unreal.

How could I watch her enjoying life so much, and not break down at this terrible knowledge? Many times I did falter, but thankfully my strength was always great whenever I was with Clare. The inevitability of the situation had me panic stricken. It was like standing on a beach and trying to stop the waves coming in with my bare hands. And all through this Clare was her usual self. She was never a problem. A very courageous child who never complained of the treatment she had to endure.

I stand tall knowing that I endured all this to give Clare her chance of life. I love her above all things, and am proud and privileged to have had her as my daughter.

John Gosney

MY PRECIOUS DAUGHTER

I love you my precious daughter,
I always have and always will,
Your smile and loving ways are with me still.

You were a smasher, a magical child,
The sight of you made my heart swell,
Where do I go from here, no one can tell.

John Gosney

THEIR COURAGE

CHRISTINE, MY DAUGHTER

Christine had Cystic Fibrosis and that's a fact. Christine did not suffer her illness and that's also a fact, because she fought her illness every second of every minute of every hour of every day.

She fought her illness with all her strength, both spiritual and physical, and when she died her spiritual strength was as strong as ever but her physical strength failed her.

Christine's strength came from the love of the people who surrounded her. Her church, family and friends, and in fact anyone who knew her. In return she touched each person she met with a special gift of happiness.

The day Christine stopped breathing was the day I stopped living. That was six months ago.

I felt very inadequate in my grief. I believe that one reason for this was because I was never a very religious person, and I thought that because Bob was, that he could understand it all better than I could. He had the same strength as Christine, whereas all I wanted to know was, *why?*

I thought I couldn't cope because I wasn't religious and didn't have that insight, but who have I talked to all the way through this? Well, Christine, but only with God's help can she get me through. Because my friends loved her so much they have shown each in their own way their love for me, and they are gradually restoring the balance in my life.

Results so far? Talking about Christine happily, remembering all the fun things about her, knowing with her guidance I will one day recover from this, and survive to be the person I once was. In a way other things are beginning to fill the void, things I don't feel guilty about, but things I know Christine would be proud of her Mum doing. And in a way, although only six months on, I believe she has brought me through to the recovery stage, but I make no excuses for slipping back sometimes.

I hope it will be a different story in twelve months' time.

Dot Ellis

69

MY FRIEND SAMMI

I remember Sammi
Her courage, her iron will.
Her illness is defeating her
But on she battles still.
Her life has hardly started,
So many things to do,
Her destiny is elsewhere,
Her spirit will see her through.
Her life will not be wasted,
She's taught us many things,
To battle on regardless,
No matter what it brings.
I hope to see her whole again,
Once we have learned our fate,
To life renewed eternal
When we have passed the gate.

Anne Alexander

THE TWO HILLS

Like a flaring, fizzling fuse
On a dank day
She reminded us of light,
Bringing warmth
She shook our half-lives awake.

On that first great climb
Up that first hill,
Up those unforgiving steps,
Unaided,
Her ashen face proclaimed
A determined defiance,
We cried inwardly,
So proud of her,
Ourselves ashamed
For taking life for granted.

Step by painful step
She climbed right to the top
Of that first great hill,
Lighting it, a frail, bright beacon,
Blinding fate
For a while.

Then, that glorious year,
That whole, hectic, happy
Life forcing
Concentration of Joy
Was an inspiration
Was a full-life lived
Was Claire.

She detonated the rock hard
Face of boredom,
Declared war on greyness,
On simulated experience,
And enjoyed life,
And we loved her.

The second hill
Was too high,
She was exhausted,
Worn out
From all that living,
From all that giving,
From all that climbing,
From all that fighting,
And hard cruel fate
Took her revenge
On one who dared
Stick out a determined
Little chin and win,
For a while.

You cannot breathe
On wind battered heights,

On sleet spattered summits,
But here in the silent
Valley, far from storms,
You can rest, Claire,
At last in peace,
Having lived
As few of us have learned to live.

Geoff Wilde

A tribute to Claire Stapleton written by her teacher.

WHEN

When you have seen your child battle against overwhelming
    disease,
When you have watched your child struggle to maintain dignity
    against debilitation,
When you have shared your child's victory over her fears,
When you have witnessed all this and known that it is for you,
That your child faces her destiny with courage,
So that you may be spared the anguish of seeing her suffer,
Then you have had a glimpse of perfection,
And perhaps seen God shining through your child.

Marilyn Shawe

FRIGHTENED EYES

Frightened eyes are like a candle flame,
Blown out before its time,
Frightened eyes see a smile again,
In the memory of their child.

Frightened eyes, like a candle flame,
Are petrified they're going to fail.
Frightened eyes can never express the pain
That they feel since that day.

72

I've got to go on, I've got to be strong;
In spite of you, because of you!
You're part of me,
And some day we will be free!
No more frightened eyes.

Frightened eyes, like a candle,
Begin to flicker in the wind.
Frightened eyes, reaching out with love,
Touch your heart long after the end.

Frightened eyes, like a candle flame,
Are a beacon to the lost.
Frightened eyes point to the hopeful way;
Cherished memories not the cost.

Yes I can go on, now that I am strong;
Because of you, not in spite of you.
Now that you're free; together we are one.

John Garrett

A CERTAIN SOMETHING

SOMETHING TO THINK ABOUT

Reflecting upon the life of my own son, Paul, and listening to the other parents at the Alder Centre, it seems to me that these children we have been lucky enough to have known and loved, have all had a special quality about them, 'a certain something' which made them so endearing.

I wonder, buried deep inside their minds, did they know that they only had a limited time here on earth? Perhaps they only needed that short length of time that they had, to learn some particular lesson. We are taught that life is eternal, but if this is so, eternity does not just start now, it must also cover the past. We tend to regard this earthly life as a beginning and an end, but maybe this life here on earth is just a training ground, a kind of apprenticeship, to see how we cope with the circumstances which may arise. To me this line of thought opens up whole new horizons. I feel very privileged to have been chosen as Paul's mother and so grateful for all the wonderful times we had together as a family before he had to leave.

Rose Foster

BEREAVEMENT

The freezing conditions of early bereavement that numb the inner man, and that feeling of terrible reality when you first wake from the night-time limbo, and realise, 'Yes, it has happened'. This for me was the first stage.

A feeling of not being in control, and of having a hair trigger stability that I could lose at any time, and for any reason, was the next stage. I could be feeling able to cope and exist one moment, the next, there was no point in trying any more.

Just before these bad periods I would always follow the same pattern, I would feel very anxious, have butterflies in my stomach, and find keeping still impossible. When these things started I knew I was about to slip into the abyss.

I didn't even notice the change to the next stage, it was so gradual. But I am now in what (for the want of a better term) I call my serene stage, whereby I can watch the world go by, and have this feeling that nothing of this world can touch me. I am insulated from it. This stage is comfortable for me, and I feel that I can have some measure of control over events happening around me.

A feeling of closeness with Clare is something I am beginning to feel. But the impression I have is not of the Clare I remember, she somehow feels mature and seems to help me get through the days. The nearest way I can describe this sensation is of oneness, as though the two of us are now one in me.

John Gosney

MY DAUGHTER, MY FRIEND

It's not so much the child in you I miss,
It's the very specialness of you,
It's the way you cared, your hug, your kiss,
That's so hard to do without.

It's the way you had of coming home,
Full of smiles and warmth and love,
You brightened the room by just being there,
It was so good to be your mum.

You had a way of sharing your joy in life,
That made me feel part of you,
You told me your plans, your dreams, your hopes,
Always looking for worthwhile things to do.

Your giving, your sharing, your caring of others,
Always there to offer your help.
I still hear your voice, so capable and pert,
'Leave it to me, mum, I'll do it'.

You loved to help, to organise, to care,
You tried to take burdens from me,
I was so grateful, so humbled,
My dearest daughter, my friend,
I thought you would always be there.

It's not so much that you had to die,
It's because you are on your own,
I want so much to hold your hand,
And follow you into that great unknown.

Marilyn Shawe

RESTING WITH SAM

My baby Sam
Today I caught you in my silent space
My forever piece of time.
Sat cross legged rocking you . . .
From side to side to side,
Soothing you.
You enfold me in these loving thoughts Sam
I watch your face, stroke the nape of your neck,
Your strawberry blonde hair
Your eyes slowly blink
With a Sam only sent expression of pleasure and love.

Jill Jones

Written a week after what would have been Sam's fourth birthday. Sam was always like a new-born baby. He was severely brain damaged at birth. Born 17.4.88, he died 25.7.90.

TRIBUTE TO A DAUGHTER

I lay in the bath last night, and watched the tears streaming down the window. Even the house seems to miss her. And why should it not? Her laughter bounced off its walls, her voice rang round its rooms, and her love was everywhere.

All those wonderful happy sounds have gone now. It is so quiet.
But her love, that beautiful emotion, that gave meaning to my life, she left behind. And that love will sustain and fill me, through the empty years or days that are left of my life.

John Gosney

THE ABSENT ONE

I feel your breath, I know you're there,
A whiff of scent, a brush of hair.
You never left, of that I'm glad.
It makes me happy, though mostly sad.

Your hair of gold, your eyes azure,
You are still around, of that I'm sure.
You brought me joy as well as pain,
I would endure it all again.

Now you're free to dance and hop,
To flit around and never stop.
To laugh and sing, skip and tease,
Do whatever comes to please.

No earthly bonds to tie you down,
No morbid thoughts to make you frown.
Your soul is strong and you are free,
Please hover on and wait for me.

Anne Alexander

ONE DAY WE'LL BE TOGETHER

KIRSTIE JANE

She lives in the wind
In amongst the trees,
Is that her voice
I hear on the breeze?

Her hair like the sun
Has a golden hue
With slivers of light
Against the background of blue.

She kicks up the leaves,
Plays with the storms,
Has several disguises,
Adopts many forms.

A whispered breath,
The lightest of touch,
Is all that I ask,
It is not too much.

One day she'll surround me,
And utter with glee:
'Come join in the wonders
Come, come with me.'

Anne Alexander

GOODNIGHT

Goodnight, my dear loved ones,
It was not meant to be.
I am now to live my life
In a land that you can't see.

This land is very beautiful,
All sunshine and no rain,
Where everybody's healthy
And no one can feel pain.

You see, heaven like earth needs children
To laugh and sing and play
To be loved by all around them
Bringing joy to every day.

So now you know I'm happy
Growing up like you want me to.
Please mention my name with a smile
And I'll send all my love to you.

Remember I'll always be near you
For your child I'll always remain,
So live your life knowing I care
And I'll be waiting when we meet again.

Bet Erickson

Written by Bet, a ward clerk at Liverpool Maternity Hospital, as though she were the baby.

A LETTER TO MATTHEW AND CHRISTOPHER

Our precious boys, this should have been our first Christmas with you, but now it is to be our first Christmas without you.

How will we get through it as we watch all the lucky families together with their children, their laughter surrounding them as they open their presents.

In your home, Matthew and Christopher, there will be none of this, just pain-filled memories of how our first Christmas together should have been.

When you died all our hopes and dreams we had for you went with you. All the things we had planned for you are now no more. Yet the love we have for you remains, it will never die, but just grows stronger and stronger for every day we are without you.

Your daddy and I love you with all our hearts and we will always love you. How we wish we could have held you in our arms, have seen your eyes, heard you laugh, listened to your cries, then comforted you. Your daddy and I will never know any of these pleasures because God took you from us as soon as you were born, for what reason we will never probably know.

But one thing is certain and that is one day we will all be together for ever and then we can try to make up for all our lost time and opportunities.

Until then, our beautiful babies, we will cling to our treasured memories of the short time we had together.

Sleep peacefully Matthew and Christopher. We love you. Mummy and Daddy.

Cathy and Simon Tinsley

YOUR SMILE, AMANDA

And as the rising sun's rays come into view
Bathing the land with their golden touch
My heart is filled with joy as I think of you,
Your warming smile that I miss so much.

Your helping hand was there with love,
Your willingness to offer and share.
No need to ask or hint or shove,
Your loving touch was always there.

These memories so very strong
Are with me all my days,
Your smile, your voice, for which I long,
Your loving, caring ways.

But now your earthly life is past,
To hug, to hold, has gone for sure.
The physical void that now must last,
I hold you in my mind once more.

You're now eternal, knowing all,
With new body from the start,
These things I just can't comprehend
But feel within my heart.

How will I know it's you, my one,
In just that little while?
I believe as Mary knew her Son,
I'll know you by your smile.

And as the sun sinks once again,
My heart feels sad with grief,
For now I must endure the pain
'Til we're united, that's my belief.

Keith Shawe

TREAT US LIKE LOST CHILDREN

THOUGHTS FROM THE OTHER SIDE

We don't know what to say to you. We don't even dare imagine the pain and hurt we are about to cause you, when we break the bad news. Most of us don't even have any personal experience of death, only that of being one step removed from your grief.

Most of us feel the need to say something to you, something that will take away the hurt, make the pain less and yet we know, deep down, nothing will, right at that moment.

That's when the mistakes happen. Those awful fidgity moments and the mind-numbing platitudes that slip out.

A whole tumble of emotions hits us too, when we have to tell you your loved one has died in our care. Most of us are in this job for our love of people and the care and help we can provide and yet death almost negates that care. Did we fail? Could we have done more? There are plenty of 'what if's and 'if only's on our part too. Only by time, experience and even personal loss, will we ever start to comprehend how you might be feeling.

We're working hard at it ... death is no longer the taboo subject it was fifteen years ago when I started my training.

Please remember, we do feel every loss, they weren't just another patient or the chap on trolley 1! To us, they were the most important person in our care at that moment and the love and care they received up to their death reflected that.

Maybe, with your help and advice, we can now prolong that care *to you* the people left behind. Where do we go from here? What do you want?

Diane E. Clarke

Diane works in the accident and emergency department at Bolton Royal Infirmary and has visited the Alder Centre.

A LETTER TO THE OTHER SIDE

Dear Diane

I was horrified to get your letter. In the five years since my son died I have only occasionally thought about the ambulance staff, police outriders, doctors and nurses who did all they could to keep my son alive.

I have been preoccupied with my own emotional stress and have not considered that those same people are still trying to do the impossible every day, and only occasionally succeeding. I have not seriously thought about the empty disappointment of 'not quite managing it' over and over again, the doubts and anxieties about one's vocation and whether one is 'suited to the job'. I hope you believe that 'God loves a trier'. I hope you give yourselves full credit when you do bring someone back from the edge because each success is priceless.

You ask 'what more can you do'. I don't think it's fair to ask much more. You know as well as I do that there is no good way to give bad news. Gentle words don't humanise brutal facts. A newly bereaved parent is inconsolable and no amount of cups of tea or soft furnishings can cushion the unacceptable.

Treat us like lost children! We are stunned by the enormity of the loss and can't think of anything else. Leave us for a little while, maybe, but be around. We are in an unfamiliar world. This is your domain. You know about the systems and practices and you are thinking more clearly than we are.

Please don't expect yourselves to soften the blow. No one can! You already do all that your training and personal skill allow. Being there, giving practical help, however basic, is enough. Don't take anything we say personally and accept that we are grateful for your help even if we appear to ignore it.

Please allow me to thank you for the policemen, ambulance and hospital staff who tried. I know your name. I will never know theirs.

Charles O'Hara